The Birdwatcher

Stephen Speight

The Birdwatcher

Ernst Klett Sprachen
Stuttgart

Stephen Speight

The Birdwatcher

1. Auflage   1   15 14 13 12 11 | 2028 27 26 25 24

Nachfolger von ISBN 3-12-570310-7

Alle Drucke dieser Auflage sind unverändert und können im Unterricht nebeneinander verwendet werden.
Die letzte Zahl bezeichnet das Jahr des Druckes. Das Werk und seine Teile sind urheberrechtlich geschützt. Jede Nutzung in anderen als den gesetzlich zugelassenen Fällen bedarf der vorherigen schriftlichen Einwilligung des Verlags.

© Ernst Klett Sprachen GmbH, Stuttgart, 1989.
Alle Rechte vorbehalten. Die Nutzung der Inhalte für Text- und Data-Mining ist ausdrücklich vorbehalten und daher untersagt.
www.klett-sprachen.de

Satz: Satzkasten, Stuttgart
Illustrationen: Julia Robinson
Umschlaggestaltung: Elmar Feuerbach
Titelbild: Alamy Images / David Forster
Druck und Bindung: Digitaldruck Tebben GmbH, Biessenhofen

Printed in Germany
ISBN 978-3-12-570312-4

Contents

The beige caravan 6
In the reed-beds 12
The woman in the motor boat 16
Stolen paintings 21
At Glemham Hall 26
Time to tell the police 30
The colonel and his daughter 37

Comprehension questions 44

The beige caravan

This year the Fullers went to White House Beach near Kessingland for their holidays. Kessingland is a small village on the east coast. The Fullers are in the Caravan Club. They read about the White House Beach caravan site in their club handbook, and thought it sounded nice.

Their caravan was in the small field next to the beach. Mr and Mrs Fuller slept at one end of the caravan, their two sons, Chris and Mark, at the other. Their twelve-year-old daughter Becky had a small tent.

The year before everyone slept in the caravan, and Becky didn't like it. Her two brothers gave her a hard time. The tent was her own idea. She needed somewhere a bit quiet now and then. In the daytime she was with her family, but in the evening she went out to the tent, turned on her small electric light, and felt very much at home. She even liked the sound of rain on the tent roof. And it rained a lot that summer. There were one or two fine days at the start of the holiday, but then the bad weather came. It didn't rain all day, but it rained every day for a few hours. And it always started at a bad time – just when the Fullers were having breakfast outside, or just when they got down to the beach.

On the fourth day of their holiday, it was raining when they woke up. Becky ran to the site shop for bread, milk and a newspaper. She was very wet when she got back to the caravan. The family was just starting breakfast.

---

0 **beige** [beɪʒ] – 3 **east coast** [ˈiːstˈkəʊst] Ostküste – 5 **caravan site** [ˈkærəvæn] Campingplatz (für Wohnwagen) – 6 **sound nice** [saʊnd] sich gut anhören – 10 **daughter** [ˈdɔːtə] Tochter – 15 **quiet** [ˈkwaɪət] ruhig – 18 **even** [ˈiːvən] sogar – 27 **wake up** [ˈweɪkʌp] aufwachen

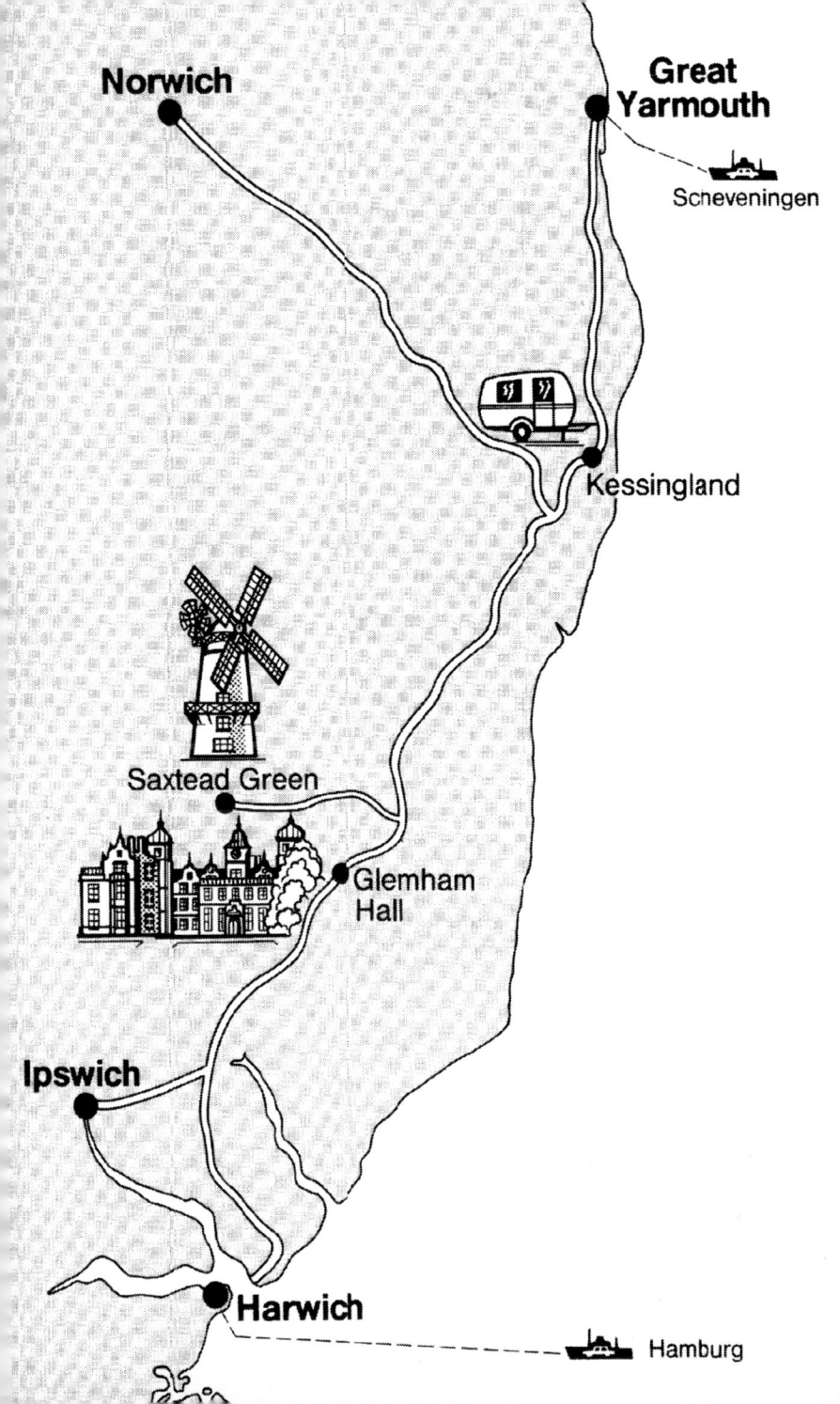

"Well." Mrs Fuller said brightly. "What shall we do today? Shopping in Norwich, or a ride along the coast?"

"I don't want to sit in the car all day," Chris said.

"Shopping is awful in the rain," Mark said.

"Let's go for a nice long walk, then."

"Oh, no, not another walk!" the children said.

"How about you, Jim?"

Mr Fuller was reading the newspaper.

"What? Oh, yes, I think that's a very good idea."

"What's a very good idea?"

"Well, what you just said is a very good idea."

"What did I say?"

"I – er – I don't know, darling."

"Great! I'm going for a walk, and you four can wash up!"

When Mrs Fuller came back from her walk, a German caravan was just arriving on the site. The car and caravan stopped near the Fullers.

"Perhaps they need some help, Jim," Mrs Fuller said. "They'll be all right. The site isn't on a hill."

"You're very lazy today. Boys, go out and help! Look, they need a push, and they've got a son – somebody for you to play with."

But the boys were playing Monopoly, and they didn't want to go and help.

"I'll get Becky, then."

Becky was watching from her tent. She went across to the German caravan with her mother.

"Hello, can we help?" Mrs Fuller asked.

---

1 **brightly** ['braɪtlɪ] fröhlich – 1 **shall** [ʃæl] sollen – 2 **Norwich** ['nɒrɪtʃ] – 14 **darling** ['dɑːlɪŋ] – 22 **lazy** ['leɪzɪ] faul – 24 **somebody** ['sʌmbɒdɪ] jemand

"Oh, yes please. We want to push the caravan back a bit, and it's stuck. The ground is very muddy here."

"Yes, it is – we've had a lot of rain."

Soon the German caravan was in the right place. The German family said thank you, then they went inside to make a cup of coffee. Mrs Fuller and Becky went back to their own caravan. It was still raining.

Suddenly everyone was asking questions.

"What are they like?"

"Do they speak English?"

"Where are they from?"

"What's their name?"

"I'm not going to tell you. You didn't want to help!"

In the afternoon the rain stopped and the sun came out. Becky and the two boys went out to play cricket. The German car drove off into town, but the boy wasn't in it. Becky walked across to the German caravan and knocked on the door. She was a bit worried. The boy opened the door. He looked a bit worried, too. "Would you like to play cricket with us?" Becky asked. "Okay, I'll be out with you in a few seconds."

"Why did you ask him to play?" Chris asked. "They don't play cricket in Germany."

"Well, he can learn, can't he!"

But the German boy *could* play cricket. He told them that he had a German father and an English mother. He didn't play cricket in school, but he often played a bit on holiday. He said his name was Mike – an easy name in German or English. His

2 **ground** [graʊnd] Boden – 20 **knock** [nɒk] klopfen

second name was Schröder. That wasn't so easy for the Fullers.

An hour later they were all tired. They sat down on camping chairs and had a drink of lemonade.

5 "Hey, what was that?" Becky said.

"What?" Chris asked. "I didn't see anything."

"There was a flash. It came from that beige caravan over there." "Well? Mark," Becky asked. "What did you see?"

10 "There's a man in there with a pair of binoculars. They're flashing in the sun."

"What's he looking at?"

"Well, I think he's looking out to sea."

3 **tired** [ˈtaɪəd]] müde – 7 **flash** [flæʃ] Blitz – 10 **binoculars** [bɪˈnɒkjʊləz] Fernglas

"Perhaps he's a birdwatcher," Chris said.

"I've read that there are some interesting birds here," Mike said.

"Yes," Chris said. "But most of them are in the reed-beds south of here."

"Well, there's a boat out there," Mike said. "Perhaps he's just looking at that."

"I noticed something funny in his van," Mark said. "He's got some big cardboard tubes in there. Why would anybody go on holiday with a van full of cardboard tubes?"

---

5 **reed-bed** [ˈriːdbed] Schilf(gürtel) – 5 **south** [saʊθ] Süden, südlich – 9 **cardboard tube** [ˈkɑːdbɔːdˈtjuːb] Papprolle – 10 **anybody** [ˈenɪbɒdɪ] (irgend) jemand

In the reed-beds

Becky woke up early next morning. One wall of her tent was yellow in the morning sun. She kicked off her sleeping bag. It was nearly too warm in the tent. Great! A fine day. She opened the door of her tent a bit and looked out. The sun was shining on the wet grass. There was a nice early morning smell in the air. Everything was quiet. No one else was moving. She decided to go down to the beach for a swim.

Becky was only in the water for ten minutes. It was very cold. She ran back up to the site with her towel round her. On the way she stopped at the site shop to buy milk and a newspaper. "Up early," the woman said.

"Yes, it's so nice to see the sun."

"Let's hope it stays fine – now you run back to your caravan and get some warm clothes on, young lady."

Suddenly Becky saw another flash. It was the man with the binoculars again. What was he doing?

Then a curtain moved at one end of the German caravan, and Mike's face appeared at the window. Becky pointed to the beige caravan, and they both saw another flash.

Becky went and had a quick shower. Mike was waiting for her when she came out of the showers.

"Hey," he said. "Our friend has gone for a walk. Let's follow him."

"Well, I don't know. It's breakfast time."

"But no one is moving in your caravan – or ours."

"Okay. Let's follow him – just for fun."

6 **smell** [smel] Duft – 7 **air** [eə] Luft – 8 **decide** [dɪˈsaɪd] sich entschließen – 11 **towel** [ˈtaʊəl] Handtuch – 21 **appear** [əˈpɪə] erscheinen – 24 **quick** [kwɪk] schnell – 27 **follow** [ˈfɒləʊ] folgen – 29 **ours** [aʊəz] unser

The man walked along the path at the back of the beach. He was tall and very straight, and he walked like a soldier.

"I think he's going to the reed-beds," Becky said.

"Yes – keep back – he'll see us."

"So what? Anybody can walk along this path."

The reed-beds were very beautiful. There were pools of blue water with tall reeds, white sand in between, and you could always hear the sea. You could walk for miles there and not see any people or buildings. The path zig-zagged between the reeds. The man did not look back. The children were nearly always behind some reeds, so they weren't worried that he would see them.

Now and then the man looked through his binoculars.

"He *is* a birdwatcher," Mike said.

"But there are only seagulls out there. The interesting birds are here in the reeds, or swimming in the pools. Look, I think that's a Canada Goose – why isn't he looking at it?"

"Perhaps he's waiting for a boat, then," Mike said. "A small boat could land on that little beach over there."

"Yes, but what for?"

"Well, perhaps he's some kind of smuggler."

"You watch too much television. Anyway, modern smugglers bring in drugs. They're rich men with fast cars. They stay in big hotels, not caravans."

"But that could be a very clever idea – the police wouldn't look for smugglers on the caravan site."

1 **path** [pɑːθ] Weg, Pfad – 2 **tall** [tɔːl] groß – 6 **So what?** [səʊˈwɒt] Na und? – 7 **pool** [puːl] Teich – 8 **in between** [bɪˈtwiːn] dazwischen – 11 **zig-zag** [ˈzɪɡzæɡ] (im) Zick-zack (laufen) – 18 **seagull** [ˈsiːɡʌl] Möwe – 20 **Canada Goose** [ˈkænədəˈɡuːs] Kanadagans – 27 **anyway** [ˈenɪweɪ] ohnehin, sowieso – 28 **drugs** [drʌɡz] Drogen – 29 **hotel** [həʊˈtel] – 30 **clever** [ˈklevə] schlau, klug

13

"Well, I don't know," Becky said. "He looks quite a nice man to me. Hey – what's he doing now?"

The man suddenly looked up and down the path, then pushed his way into the reeds. A few minutes later he came out again, and walked quickly back towards the caravan site. The children jumped back into the reeds. He didn't see them.

When he was gone, they ran to the place where he had disappeared into the reeds. There was a very small path, and you could see where the man had walked. A few metres into the reeds they came to a big old box, with a piece of plastic over it to keep it dry. The box was empty.

"Do you think he took something out of the box?" Mike asked. "I don't think so – anyway nothing very big. He wasn't carrying anything."

---

5 **quickly** [ˈkwɪklɪ] schnell – 6 **towards** [təˈwɔːdz] auf ... zu – 9 **disappear** [dɪsəˈpɪə] verschwinden – 13 **dry** [draɪ] trocken

"Perhaps he hoped there would be something in the box – perhaps something from a boat. But the boat didn't come, so he had to go back empty-handed."

"Mike! You really *do* watch too much television."

"Do I? He knew about that box, didn't he. Why did he go and look in it?

What's *your* idea?"

"I don't know. Come on, let's go back and have breakfast."

At the caravan site they met four worried parents.

– Where have you been?

– Are you hurt?

– Did you get lost?

– We had breakfast hours ago!

– We nearly called the police!

– Why didn't you tell us you were going out?

Becky and Mike tried to answer all the questions, said they were sorry, then went into their caravans for a late breakfast. Chris came to sit by his sister.

"Why didn't you wake me? I'm interested in the birdwatcher, too."

"I couldn't come in the caravan – I didn't want to wake Mum and Dad."

"Well, next time you could tap the window just here – that's where my head is at night."

"How do you mean, 'next time'?"

"Well, next time he goes to look in his box in the reeds."

"So you think there is something going on."

"Yes, of course I do. Don't you?"

---

13 **hurt** [hɜːt] verletzt – 21 **(be) interested in** ['ɪntrəstɪd] sich für etwas interessieren – 25 **tap** [tæp](leicht) klopfen

The woman in the motor boat

During the next few days the children were on the birdwatcher's trail. When he went for a walk, two or three of them followed him. He always looked out to sea, but no boat came to meet him. He always looked in the box, but there was never anything in it.

When he went out in his car, they noticed that he often took a camera with him. They rode after him on their bikes, but of course they lost him after a mile or two. The parents didn't ask many questions – they were quite pleased that the children had something to do.

Then, at last, something happened. The man went for a walk, but the children didn't follow him. The weather was a bit better that morning, so they played cricket. In the afternoon they wanted to go swimming. The birdwatcher wasn't much fun any more. They were tired of him.

Then the man came back. Mike saw him, and forgot all about the cricket. The ball went straight past him. He stood there with his mouth open.

"Look," he said to the others. "He's come back with a new cardboard tube."

"Don't look at him," Chris said. "Go on with the game. He'll notice that we're watching him."

The man took the tube out of his car. Becky whispered to Mark: "It says something on the tube. Get the binoculars and try to read it. Don't let him see you!"

---

1 **during** [ˈdjʊərɪŋ] während – 2 **(be) on someone's trail** [treɪl] jmd. auf der Spur (sein) – 11 **quite** [kwaɪt] ziemlich, ganz – 11 **pleased** [pliːzd] zufrieden – 13 **at last** [ətˈlɑːst] endlich – 18 **any more** [enɪˈmɔː] nicht mehr – 20 **forget/forgot** [fəˈget] vergessen – 27 **whisper** [ˈwɪspə] flüstern

Mark ran into the Fullers' caravan and watched from the window.

The man went into his caravan with the tube. It didn't look very heavy. The children went on with their game. They tried not to look at the beige caravan, but it was difficult. The man stayed in his caravan for about half an hour, then he came out again with the tube and got in his car.

The children waited until he was out of the gate.

"Right." Chris shouted. "On your bikes!"

Mark ran out of the caravan.

"I want to come, too. Wait for me! Don't you want to know what it said on the tube?"

Becky waited for him.

"Well, Mark, what did it say?"

"It said COPY 20. What does that mean?"

"I don't know, Mark. Perhaps he's going to make twenty copies of something. Come on – we'll lose the others."

But they met the others just outside the site.

"We lost him," Chris said. "He was going much too fast for us."

He came back at teatime. Mark ran into the caravan to watch through the binoculars. Again he took the tube into his caravan. "It says something else on the tube now," Mark said. "He's put a line through COPY. It says ORIG 20."

"Oh dear," Becky said. "It's still a puzzle. Has anybody else got an idea?" Then the man came out of his caravan with the tube, and walked towards the reed-beds.

"Run and get Mike," Chris said to Becky. "Come on Mark, this could be interesting."

"Just a minute, Chris," his Mum said. "It's your turn to wash up."

"Mum, *please!*" Chris said.

"Well, all right – but it'll be your turn twice tomorrow."

The children followed the man to the reed-beds. He went straight to the box, and came back without the tube. The children hid in the reeds. When he was out of the way they came out, and walked toward the place where the box was hidden.

"I'm worried," Mark said. "What if he comes back?"

"I'll stay out here on the path," Mike said. "If someone comes, I'll tell you."

"Okay – thanks, Mike." Becky said.

Mike hid in the reeds next to the path. The others pushed their way through to the box. They could see the cardboard tube through the plastic.

---

9 **puzzle** [ˈpʌzl] – 16 (**it's your**) **turn** [tɜːn] (du bist) dran – 18 **twice** [twaɪs] zweimal – 22 **hide/hid** [haɪd] sich verstecken – 31 **through** [θru] durch

"Let's look inside the tube," Becky said.
"No," Mark said, "It could be dangerous."
"What do you think, Chris?" Becky asked.
"Well. I don't think it's dangerous, but ... well, it isn't ours, is it."
"Perhaps it's stolen. Anyway, we're only going to look."
"Okay then. I'll pull back the plastic for you," Chris said. "You can open it."
Becky was just trying to open the tube when Mike crashed through the reeds. They all jumped.
"Quick," Mike whispered. "A motor boat has just come in over there. A woman is coming this way."
The children hid in the reeds. Suddenly it was very quiet.
"She'll hear my heart!" Mark said. "It's going like a steam engine."

11 **crash through** [ˈkræʃˈθruː] durchbrechen – 16 **heart** [hɑːt] Herz – 17 **steam engine** [ˈstiːmˈendʒɪn] Dampfmaschine

"No, she won't," Becky said. "Only you can hear it."

Then Becky noticed something. The plastic wasn't straight. She ran out and pulled at it. She was only just back behind the reeds when the woman appeared. She had another cardboard tube under her arm. They could read what it said on the side: COPY 21. The woman was about twenty-five. She was wearing jeans and an anorak, and she had short blonde hair. She looked very worried.

"I think she heard something," Mark whispered. "Perhaps she knows we're here."

"Ssh!"

The woman didn't move for four or five minutes. She just waited and listened. At last she pulled the plastic off the box, and changed the cardboard tubes. She put back the plastic and again waited for a long time. Becky wanted to sneeze, but she held her nose between finger and thumb. The sneeze didn't come. Then the woman went back to her boat, and a few minutes later the children came out of the reeds. They didn't look inside the tube. They were too frightened. They thought the birdwatcher could come at any minute. They sat down outside the Fullers' caravan and had a cold drink.

"I noticed something interesting," Becky said.

"Oh?"

"The woman had paint on her hands."

"Perhaps she's painting her boat," Chris said.

"Green, yellow and red? What colour was the boat, Mike?"

"White, with a blue line round it."

"So she's painting something else. I wonder what it is."

18 **sneeze** [sniːz] niesen – 19 **thumb** [θʌm] Daumen – 23 **be frightened** [ˈfraɪtənd] Angst haben – 33 **wonder** [ˈwʌndə] sich fragen

Stolen paintings

Next morning it was Becky's turn to buy milk and a newspaper again. On the way back she looked at the front page. The main news was about the queen's trip to Australia, but down near the bottom of the page Becky saw something very interesting. This is what she read:

Paintings stolen from stately homes

Police in the east of England are looking for "Colonel Limp". He visits stately homes and steals valuable paintings. He always puts a fake painting in place of the real one, so it is often months before anyone notices that a painting is missing. But then people remember a tall visitor who looked like a colonel. The guide in one stately home said that the "colonel" has a limp.

Visitors go round the houses in groups. How does the "colonel" find time to change the paintings? Where does he get the fakes from? What does he do with the stolen paintings?

It won't be easy to catch him. As a guide at another stately home said: "A lot of our visitors look like colonels."

Becky was very excited. She ran all the way back to the caravan. "Hey, look at this!" she said. Everyone read the article. "Well?" Becky said. "What do you think?"

---

4 **Australia** [ɒ'streɪlɪə] – 7 **painting** ['peɪntɪŋ] Gemälde – 7 **stately home** ['steɪtlɪ'həʊm] Herrenhaus – 9 **colonel** ['kɜːnəl] Oberst – 9 **(to have a) limp** [lɪmp] humpeln – 9 **visit** ['vɪzɪt] besuchen – 10 **valuable** ['væljʊəbl] wertvoll – 11 **fake** [feɪk] Fälschung – 13 **remember** [rɪ'membə] sich erinnern – 13 **visitor** ['vɪzɪtə] Besucher – 14 **guide** [gaɪd] Führer – 20 **catch** [kætʃ] fangen

"What do you mean, what do we think?" Chris asked. "It's an interesting story, but so what?"

"Boys! You can't put two and two together. I think our birdwatcher is this colonel. He's got paintings in the cardboard tubes. The woman we saw yesterday was bringing him a new fake. He'll take it to a stately home somewhere and swap it for the real painting."

"But this 'colonel' hasn't got a limp," Mrs Fuller said. "I think you're putting two and two together and making five. Come on everybody, breakfast. It's not a bad day, and we want to get down to the beach."

Becky went down to the beach with the others, but she didn't enjoy herself. She was thinking about the birdwatcher and the colonel all the time. She played cricket for a while, but when the ball came to her, she was looking out to sea.

"Wake up, Becky!" Chris called.

"Sorry – I'll go and get it." Becky ran and picked up the ball. On the way back she saw that the birdwatcher was sitting near the top of the beach. She threw the ball to the others and went back to her parents.

"Dad," she asked, "Did you bring down the binoculars?" "Yes – they're in the beach bag."

Becky got out the binoculars, then she lay down on the sand behind the beach bag, and looked at the birdwatcher. He was reading a newspaper – it was the same as the one Becky had bought that morning. The paper was open, so he wasn't reading he front page at the moment. Then he closed the paper and looked at the front page.

---

7 **swap** [swɒp] tauschen – 15 **enjoy** [ɪnˈdʒɔɪ] sich amüsieren – 27 **lie/lay down** [laɪ][leɪ] sich hinlegen

"I just know he's reading that story," Becky thought.

She went across to Mike's family and sat down next to Mike. He didn't know about the story in the paper yet. When Becky told him about it, he was on her side – but not as sure as she was.

"The others think I'm silly," Becky said. "We need some real evidence."

"I know," Mike said. "We could watch his caravan all evening. If he's this colonel, I'm sure he'll do something suspicious." "He has done a lot of suspicious things," Becky said. "What about the box in the reeds, the woman in the boat, and the cardboard tubes. He must be the colonel."

"Well, let's watch him this evening, and perhaps we'll find out." After tea the two children hid behind some bushes and watched the beige caravan. The man had his tea, then he read the paper for a bit. He looked at the front page, but only for a few seconds. Then he washed up.

"Not very suspicious so far," Becky said.

"It's still early," Mike said. "Wait and see."

Then the man picked up a book and started to read. Mike had a look through the binoculars.

"Can you see what the book is about?" Becky asked. "No – it's too dark."

The man thought it was dark, too. He turned on the light. "Can you see anything now?" Becky asked.

"Yes. It says *Stately Homes* in *East Anglia*."

"There!" Becky said. "He's finding out where he can steal some more valuable paintings."

"Or he's just planning to go and look at a stately home," Mike said.

---

6 **sure** [ʃɔː] sicher – 8 **evidence** ['evɪdens] Beweise – 11 **suspicious** [səˈspɪʃəs] verdächtig – 17 **bush(es)** [bʊʃ] [ˈbʊʃɪz] Busch, Gebüsch – 30 **East Anglia** [ˈiːstˈæŋɡlɪə]

"A lot of people do that on holiday."

The man picked up a pencil and drew a line under something in the book.

"Do you think he's just on an ordinary holiday?" Becky asked. "No, not really. Something funny is going on."

After a while the man put down his book and looked at his watch.

Then he got up and turned on his television.

"It's nine o'clock – time for the news on BBC One," Becky said. "Well, most people watch the news – that's not very suspicious, is it!"

Then, suddenly, half way through the news the man started to laugh.

The children couldn't see what he was watching.

"I'll run back and see what's on the news," Becky said.

The Fullers weren't watching TV. Becky turned on, but the newsreader was talking about a bad road accident. She ran across to the Schröders' caravan.

"Excuse me," she said. "Are you watching the BBC news?" "Yes. Why?"

"Well, we're watching the birdwatcher – and he's watching the news, too. He suddenly started to laugh in the middle. Was there something funny?

"No – it's about a car accident at the moment." Mr Schröder said.

"What was on before that?"

"Something about house prices, I think."

"No – that was earlier," Mrs Schröder said. "There was something about a colonel who steals paintings from stately homes." "Thanks. That's what I wanted to know."

---

4 **ordinary** [ˈɔːdɪnəri] gewöhnlich – 5 **not really** [ˈrɪəli] eigentlich nicht – 10 **BBC One** [ˈbiːˈbiːˈsiː ˈwʌn] „1. Programm" – 25 **middle** [ˈmɪdl] Mitte

Becky ran back to Mike.

"Well?" he asked.

"There was a report about the colonel."

"Really? Why do you think our man laughed?"

"Because he is the colonel, and he thinks he's being very clever."

"Well, you could be right."

"We must tell the police."

"They'll laugh too – at us! We still haven't got any evidence." "I'll talk to Mum and Dad in the morning," Becky said. "We'll follow him in the car next time he goes out."

"We'll come too – Mum and Dad both read detective stories on holiday. I know they'll be interested in the real thing."

14 **detective** [dɪˈtektɪv]

At Glemham Hall

Mike and Becky both talked to their parents. The Fullers said they would follow the birdwatcher in their car the next time he went out, and of course they would take Mike, too. The Schröders would stay on the site and make lunch for Chris and Mark.

They wanted to go fishing – the birdwatcher wasn't so interesting after all.

The man didn't go out next day. But at half past eight the next morning he put a cardboard tube in the back of his car and drove away. The Fullers hadn't finished breakfast yet. They left everything on the table and jumped in the car. Becky ran across and tapped on Mike's door. He came out, half in his clothes and half in his pyjamas. They got to the main road just in time – they could still see the birdwatcher's car. He was driving south along the A12.

The Fullers had some information leaflets in the car. You could get leaflets in the office on the caravan site. Becky looked through them.

"He could be on his way to Glemham Hall," she said after a while. "It's down here on the A12."

Suddenly the man turned right.

"Oh well," Mr Fuller said. "So much for that idea. Are there any big houses along this road, Becky?"

Becky looked through the leaflets again, but she couldn't find anything.

Mrs Fuller had the map book.

---

0 **Glemham Hall** [ˈgleməm ˈhɔːl] (a stately home) – 8 **after all** [ˈɑːftər ɔːl] schließlich – 15 **pyjamas** [pɪˈdʒɑːməz] – 16 **main road** [ˈmeɪnˈrəʊd] Hauptstraße

"There's a windmill at Saxtead Green," she said. "I can't see anything else."

"Can I see the map, please?" Mike asked from the back seat. He looked at the map for a while.

"Perhaps he's seen us," Mike said. "He hopes we'll think he's going somewhere else – then he'll go back to this Hall. There are lots of little roads round here."

"Well," Mr Fuller said, "you could be right. But he's got to get away from us if he wants to do that – or we'll just follow him all the way back to the Hall."

They drove round the next corner – and the birdwatcher's blue Maestro was gone.

"Which way?" Mr Fuller asked, "Left, right, or straight on?" "We don't know," Becky said. "Let's drive straight back to this Hall – perhaps he'll be there."

And he was – well, his car was. The Fullers and Mike bought tickets and looked round the house, but they couldn't find the birdwatcher – or the colonel – anywhere. There were a lot of paintings in Glemham Hall, but of course they all looked all right. You couldn't go right up to them because there was a rope in front. Becky bought a little book about the house, with copies of some of the paintings in it. Mike went up to the guide.

"Did you read this story about a 'colonel' who steals paintings?" he asked.

"No – and what I read is none of your business."

The guide was a big, very straight man. He looked like a colonel.

---

1 **windmill** ['wɪndmɪl] Windmühle – 1 **Saxtead Green** ['sæksted 'gri:n] – 14 **Maestro** ['maɪstrəʊ] (brit. Auto der Rover-Gruppe) – 22 **not anywhere** ['enɪweə] nirgendwo – 25 **rope** [rəʊp] Seil – 30 **it's none of your business** ['bɪznɪs] es geht dich nichts an

"It was on the TV news, too," Mike said. "We think this man is staying on our caravan site. His car is outside Glemham Hall at this moment."

"Oh, really. Which painting has he stolen, then?"

"This man puts fakes in the place of real paintings. You wouldn't see anything wrong."

"How could he change the paintings round? It would take a couple of hours, and there are hundreds of people around. Anyway, where is this 'colonel'?"

"That's the funny thing – we can't find him."

"Look, son, you're on holiday, right? Well, I'm not, so will you please go away and let me get on with my job."

When they went out to their car, the blue Maestro was still there. But the birdwatcher – or the colonel – wasn't. They drove back to the caravan site.

Chris and Mark ran up to the car.

"Well," Mark asked, "Did anything happen?"

"Not much," Becky said. "We saw his car outside this Glemham Hall place, but we didn't see him. Why isn't the tea ready?"

The birdwatcher didn't come back until the next morning. He took a cardboard tube into his caravan, and pulled the curtains. Becky looked at the beige caravan through the binoculars. "I think he's gone to bed," she said. "I wonder why he's so tired."

Then Becky noticed something very interesting. The curtains at the living room end of the man's caravan were not pulled. The top of the cardboard

8 **couple** [ˈkʌpl] ein paar

tube was against the side window – and the lid was missing.

Very, very slowly Becky crept across to the other van and looked into the tube. Then she ran back again.

"Well? What did you see?" Mark asked.

Becky was very excited.

"Just a second," she said. "Where did I put that little book with the paintings in it?"

She found the book and looked through it. Suddenly she stopped and pointed to one of the paintings.

"There," she said. "I saw a corner of that painting, *The Lady of the Lake*. I'm sure I did."

She had another look at the tube through the binoculars. The word COPY had a line through it. It now said ORIG 21.

---

1 **lid** [lɪd] Deckel – 3 **creep/crept** [kriːp] [krept] schleichen

Time to tell the police

"Time to tell the police." Mr Fuller said, when Becky told her parents about the painting in the tube.

"Can Mike come with us?" Becky asked.

"Yes, of course, but this isn't an outing, you know."

5   Mr Fuller drove down to the police station with Becky and Mike. Well, it wasn't really a police station. It was the policeman's house, and he had a little office in one of the rooms. He listened
10 carefully to the children's story.

"Right," he said. "Show me this painting in your book. I'll ring up Glemham Hall and ask them to check."

The telephone number was in the book.

15 "Hello," the policeman said. "Kessingland police here. We think someone could have stolen one of your paintings – yes, there is a boy here – oh, I see, you talked to him yesterday. And? – you think he reads too many detective stories. Yes, but someone
20 *is* stealing pictures from stately homes – and this boy's friend has seen one of your paintings in a cardboard tube on their caravan site – they know it is one of your paintings because it's in a book about Glemham Hall – yes, I'm sure you've got a
25 good alarm system, but would you please check a painting called ... just a second, *The Lady of the Lake.* Why are you laughing? – Oh, I see. Yes, right, I'll tell the children not to worry you again – Yes, I'm sure you're a very busy man. Goodbye, Sir."

---

4 **outing** [ˈaʊtɪŋ] Ausflug – 25 **alarm system** [ɔˈlɑːm sɪstəm] Alarmanlage – 29 **busy** [ˈbɪzɪ] beschäftigt

The young policeman put down the phone. He looked very hot. "Phew!" he said, and smiled at the children. "That guide was very angry with you – and with me. I hope someone *has* ... No, I mustn't say that!"

"Why did the guide laugh?" Becky asked.

"Well, when I told him the name of the painting, he said that they have big posters of it. They sell about ten a day in the summer – in cardboard tubes."

"Oh," Mike said. "I expect you saw a poster then, Becky – not the painting."

"It *was* the painting. Remember, our man had this cardboard tube *before* he went to Glemham

---

11 **expect** [ɪkˈspekt] annehmen

Hall. And the painting in the tube was rough – not smooth like a poster. And I saw their cardboard tubes at the gift shop. They're much smaller."

The policeman listened to this, then he said.

"Well, there isn't much we can do at the moment. The guide doesn't think anyone has stolen a painting, and he doesn't want our help. What we need is some evidence."

Becky put a little plastic bag on the policeman's desk.

"There's some evidence for you," she said. The policeman picked up the bag. "What's in here, then?" He asked.

"Bits of paint," Becky said. "I went back to Glemham Hall by bus after we saw a corner of the painting."

"Chris said you were out for a long walk!" Mr Fuller said. "I'm sorry," Becky said. "But it was important. Anyway, there was a stop quite near Glemham Hall. I went in, and waited in the room with *The Lady of the Lake*. When the guide went out, I got under the rope, and looked on the floor under the painting. There were some bits of paint down there – green, red and yellow. Some looked very old – and some looked new. I pushed them into this bag with my toothbrush. I think the old bits are from the real painting, and the new bits are from the fake. And I think the birdwatcher slept all day because he was in Glemham Hall all night. He hid somewhere. Then, when everything was quiet, he took the real painting out of its frame, and put the

---

1 **rough** [rʌʃ] – 2 **smooth** [smuːð] glatt – 3 **gift shop** [ˈɡɪft ʃɒp] Souvenirladen – 31 **frame** [freɪm] Rahmen

fake in its place. Next morning he waited for some visitors to come in – and walked out with them."

"How did he hide the painting?" Mrs Fuller asked.

"I don't know, Mum – not in one of his cardboard tubes. They're too big – somebody would notice."

"Well," the policeman said. "If you're right, this is real evidence. I'll send it away for tests.

The next morning Mr Fuller drove Becky down to the policeman's house. They wanted to take Mike with them, but he wasn't there.

"Well," the policeman said. "You *were* right about those bits of paint. They really *were* evidence. Most of them were old – but one or two were new. We think these new bits are from the fake painting.

Where else could they be from? All the paintings in the Hall are old."

"So you think our birdwatcher is this Colonel Limp."

"Yes. We're going down to have a look at his caravan now. I'm just waiting for the inspector."

"Can we come and watch?"

"Of course you can – but you must stay well away from the caravan – it could be dangerous."

The inspector came with six men in two cars. They picked up the young policeman, and drove down to the caravan site. Mr Fuller and the children followed. The policemen went round to the caravans near the birdwatcher's caravan and asked people to go across to the other side of the site. One old caravanner didn't want to move.

"I want to see the action," he said. "I'm going to stay in my caravan."

"But sir," the inspector said, "he could have a gun. The walls of a caravan are very thin – a bullet would go straight through them."

"Oh – yes, I see. Well, perhaps you're right."

The old caravanner went with the others. People hid behind cars and caravans. Suddenly it was very quiet.

The inspector went across to the beige caravan and knocked on the door.

"This is the police. Open the door, please."

There wasn't a sound from inside the caravan.

"His car is there," Becky said. "I don't think he's gone out this morning."

The inspector knocked again. No answer.

19 **gun** [gʌn] Schusswaffe, Pistole – 20 **thin** [θɪn] dünn – 20 **bullet** [ˈbʊlɪt] Kugel

"Break the door down," he said to his men.
That was a very easy job for the policemen. Caravan doors are very thin, too.
Somehow Mark was there with the policemen. He had a good look before they sent him away. He ran back to the others. "He's not there – but the van is full of books about stately homes, and paintings. And I saw some plans of houses too, with crosses to show the paintings he wanted to steal. We were right!"

8 **cross** [krɒs] Kreuz(chen)

The inspector came across to the children.

"The Kessingland policeman says you kids know quite a lot about this man. He's not out in his car, so he can't be far away. Where could he be?"

Suddenly Mike was there with the others.

"He's gone to the reed-beds, sir," he said.

"How do you know?"

"Well, he goes off along a little path that no one else uses. Last night I made the sand there nice and smooth. This morning there are new footprints in it."

"Well done," the inspector said. "Where did you get the idea?" "Oh, I saw it on "Tatort" once. That's a crime show on German television."

---

2 **kids** [kɪdz] Kinder – 10 **footprint** [ˈfʊtprɪnt] Fußabdruck

The colonel and his daughter

The inspector took the Kessingland policeman with him, and Becky and Mike. The parents were worried about the colonel's gun, but the inspector smiled. "Don't worry," he said. "We only wanted to frighten that old camper a bit. We don't think our man is dangerous."

The other policemen stayed to check the birdwatcher's car and caravan.

The inspector, the young policeman and the two children ran along the main path, then turned onto the small path through the reed-beds.

"Look," Mike said. "There are the new footprints. Oh! There are more of them now. What does that mean?

They followed the footprints. Soon they were near the box in the reeds where the man hid the paintings.

Becky told the inspector about the box, and the woman in the motor boat. The four of them moved forward, one step at a time.

No one made a sound. Suddenly they saw the birdwatcher. He was waiting on the beach, with a cardboard tube under his arm. Every few seconds he looked back. You could see he was very worried.

"I think he knows we're after him," the inspector said.

"Sir, there's the motor boat," Mike said. "Look, over there." "Let's get him!" the young policeman said.

20 **forward** ['fɔːwəd] vorwärts – 20 **step** [step] Schritt

"Not so fast, George," the inspector said. "Let's wait till the woman has landed, then we'll get them both."

It seemed a very long time before the boat arrived. No one moved. No one said anything.

At last the boat came in. The woman turned off the engine and jumped out. The man walked towards her, dropped the cardboard tube and put his arms around her.

"Dad!" she said. "Is something wrong."

"Yes," the birdwatcher said. "I was worried, so I went back to the site to have a look. The police are there. I'm coming with you in the boat."

The young policeman tried to jump up. The inspector tried to stop him – and fell in a deep pool.

"Oh, sorry, sir," the young policeman said.

The birdwatcher looked round and saw them. He and the girl ran down to the boat. They left the cardboard tube on the sand. The young policeman tried to pull out the inspector, but the inspector was a big, heavy man.

"Don't let them get away!" the inspector shouted.

Becky and Mike ran towards the boat, but the colonel and his daughter were already in it. The woman pulled the rope to start the engine. It went first pull.

This time Becky remembered something from a film. The sea had brought in an old bit of blue nylon rope. There it was on the sand, near the motor boat. Becky picked it up as she ran. She went straight on into the sea and dropped the rope onto

2 **till** [tɪl] bis – 4 **seem** [siːm] scheinen

the boat's propeller. The motor stopped with a jerk. It wouldn't start again.

The man tried to push the boat off with a paddle, but Mike held the front.

5   The inspector and the policeman came down the beach. The inspector was wet and sandy, but he still

1 **propeller** [prəˈpelə] (Schiffs)Schraube – 1 **jerk** [dʒɜːk] Ruck – 6 **wet** [wet] nass

looked very important. "Right," he said. "I'm afraid this is the end of your little game."

The colonel and his daughter got out of the boat and stood on the sand together.

The young policeman picked up the cardboard tube and pulled out a painting. It was *The Lady of the Lake*, of course.

"Where were you taking that painting?" the inspector asked. "I'm not saying anything," the woman said.

"All right. We'll talk about it back at the station."

"Sir," the young policeman said.

"Well, sir. I've always lived round here, and I know something about boats. This boat is too small to go very far on the North Sea. There must be another boat waiting for them out there."

"Good man, George." The inspector took out his radio and made a quick call. The radio was wet, but it still worked.

"The helicopters will be up there in a few minutes," the inspector said. "They'll find this other boat. Are you sure you don't want to talk. Remember, we know most of the story anyway." "Well, ..." the man said.

"No, Dad, don't tell them anything," the girl said.

"It's too late, Sarah. Let me tell them. I'll feel better. Could we sit down somewhere, please? Don't worry, inspector. I'm not dangerous. And I won't try to run away."

The inspector and the man sat on an old board. The colonel told his story.

---

1 **I'm afraid** [əˈfreɪd] leider – 18 **radio** Funkgerät – 20 **helicopter** [ˈhelɪkɒptə] Hubschrauber – 23 **most of** [məʊst] das meiste

"Once I had a stately home myself. My family is as old as Robin Hood – older. We needed money. I didn't want visitors in the house, a cafeteria in the best room, and a zoo in the garden. So we had to sell the house. It was a terrible shock for all of us. A year later my wife was dead.

Sarah was always very good at art. When she left art school, we made a plan together. We found a nice painting – just one in each stately home. Sarah made a copy of it. Then I went in and changed the paintings round. We thought we could buy our house back one day."

"But that's stealing, sir," the inspector said.

"Just one painting from each house, remember. These rich people can do without one of their paintings, don't you think?

And we always gave them a very good copy. No one noticed till somebody wanted to sell one of our copies. They did some tests and found that it was a fake. Then people started looking for other fakes, and the story got into the news."

"What did you do with the stolen paintings, sir?"

"We sold them to a Dutch art dealer – the man with the big motor boat – and he sold them to private collectors for a very good price."

"Can I ask a question?" Mike asked.

"Why not," the inspector said.

"Are you really a colonel?"

"Oh yes, I'm a colonel all right."

"Did you hurt your leg in the war?"

For the first time the man laughed.

---

6 **wife** [waɪf] Ehefrau – 15 **do without** [wɪðaʊt] auf etwas verzichten – 23 **art dealer** ['ɑːt'diːlə] Kunsthändler – 25 **private** ['praɪvət] privat – 25 **collector** [kə'lektə] Sammler – 30 **war** [wɔː] Krieg

"What's all this?" the inspector asked. "I don't understand." "Well," Mike said, "the newspaper article said that the colonel had a limp."

"But he didn't have a limp on the caravan site," Becky said. "I know ..."

"Yes, young lady," the colonel said, "I think you've got it. I had to get the paintings out of the houses somehow. So I always went into the toilet and wrapped the painting round my leg. I went in without a limp, and came out next morning with a limp. The guides thought I was a different colonel."

"Very clever," said the young policeman. The inspector gave him a look.

"Will they go to prison for a long time, sir?" Becky asked. The colonel's daughter started to cry.

"I don't know," the inspector said. "How many paintings …?" "Don't worry," the colonel said. "You'll get them all back." "But we'll never get our house back," the girl said.

"I think it's a very interesting story," Becky said. "Why don't you write a book about it and earn some money – you'll have a lot of time in prison."

"And your daughter can draw the pictures," the inspector said. This time everybody laughed.

---

8 **somehow** [ˈsʌmhaʊ] irgendwie – 9 **wrap round** [ˈræpˈraʊnd] um etwas wickeln – 10 **without** [wɪðaʊt] ohne – 21 **earn** [ɜːn] verdienen

Comprehension questions

The beige caravan

Things to talk about:
– Becky and her tent
– the weather that summer
– the German caravan Mike
– the beige caravan

In the reed-beds

1. What was the man from the beige caravan like?
2. Where did he go?
3. What did he do there?
4. Why were the parents worried?

The woman in the motor boat

Try to finish the sentences:
1. The birdwatcher went ...
2. He came back with ...
3. Then he went out ...
4. The children tried to ...
5. He came back ...
6. He went to the reed-beds and ...
7. Then a woman ...
8. She changed ...
9. Becky noticed that ...

Stolen paintings

1. Say as much as you can about "Colonel Limp".
2. Has the birdwatcher done anything suspicious?
3. What did he do that evening?
4. Why do you think he laughed?

At Glemham Hall

Yes or no? Try to give a short answer – and then say a bit more.
1. Did the birdwatcher go straight to Glemham Hall?
2. Did the guide really listen to Mike?
3. Did the children see the Birdwatcher at the Hall?
4. Did he come back to his caravan that day?
5. Did Becky see something interesting in his caravan?

Time to tell the police

1. Why did the guide laugh?
2. Why did Becky think it was the real painting?
3. Why did Becky go back to the Hall?
4. Why was the Birdwatcher away all night?
5. Why were the bits of paint evidence?
6. Why did the police ask people to go across to the other side of the site?
7. Why did Mark say, "We were right!"?
8. How did Mike know that the Birdwatcher had been to the reed-beds?

The colonel and his daughter

1. Why did the inspector say "Not so fast, George."?
2. Why was the birdwatcher worried?
3. What did he want to do?
4. What happened to the inspector?
5. How did Becky stop the boat?
6. Why did the colonel start to steal paintings?
7. What did he do with the paintings?
8. Why did he sometimes limp?
9. What can the colonel and his daughter do in prison?